Copyright © 2017 by Lenn Vincent GmbH.

All rights reserved. This book or any portion thereof may not be reproduced or used in any manner whatsoever without the express written permission of the publisher except for the use of brief quotations in a book review.

First Printing, 2017

ISBN 978-3-9524827-3-5

www.leosnowpard.com

Leo Snowpard
AND HIS FIRST SCOOTER

Author
MELANIE ROEMER

Illustrations by
JUN-PIERRE SHIOZAWA

It is summer and Leo plays outside a lot with Maya and his other friends. "Come on, let's go and ride scooters," suggests Freddy Fox. "Do you have a scooter?" he asks Leo.

"No, I do not have a scooter. I've also never ridden a scooter. Is it difficult?" Leo Snowpard asks.

"No, not at all." Freddy hops on his scooter and rides away. Maya taps Leo and holds out her scooter to him, "Leo, if you like, you can ride my scooter." Leo is happy. "But before you take off, you have to put on a helmet." Maya gives Leo her helmet.

In the beginning, riding a scooter is not so easy. But Leo does not give up and after a lot of practicing, he can ride really well.
Leo and Maya alternate with their scooters and spend the whole afternoon together with their friends. Leo enjoys riding the scooter very much. He does not get tired at all.
"My mom is calling Leo, I have to go home," Maya says. "Can you give me the helmet?"
Sadly, Leo hands over the helmet to Maya. Leo Snowpard would have preferred to continue forever.
Now Leo's mom also calls, "Leo, please come in! It's time to eat dinner."

When Leo arrives home, he washes his paws and sits down at the dining table. Together with his mom, dad, and Lilly, he eats dinner. During the meal, Leo thinks about the scooter. It was a lot of fun. Lilly wonders, "Leo, why are you so quiet?" Leo Snowpard murmurs, "You know, Lilly, all the children have a scooter, but I don't have one." Lilly responds, "You can have a scooter for your birthday, Leo." "Oh, but it is a long time until my birthday," says Leo sadly and thoughtfully continues eating.

After the meal, Lilly takes Leo Snowpard to bed.

"Lilly, I have a good idea," blurts out Leo.

"I could take my money from the money box and buy my own scooter with it."

For a long time, Leo has been helping Lilly out at their Mom and Dad's company. He gets his own money for the work he does and saves it in his money box.

"That's a wonderful idea," Lilly says. "We just have to see if you have enough money in your money box," Lilly explains. "Let's go after school tomorrow to the store and see what a scooter costs?"

"Oh, yes," Leo rejoices and cuddles into his blanket.

The next day, Lilly picks up her brother Leo from school. Together they set out on the way to the scooter shop. Arriving at the shop, Leo sees his dream scooter in the shop window. It is green and has red stripes at the front. "Lilly, this is my favorite scooter," Leo says enthusiastically.

"It is really nice, Leo, but it costs $ 50.00. That's a lot of money. Let's see if we can find another one," Lilly suggests and they enter the store. "Leo, look. Here is almost the same scooter with a helmet. It only costs $ 30.00. That is much less than the one in the window," Lilly explains.

"How long do I have to save for it?" Leo asks. "Let's go home and then we'll see how much is already in your money box," Lilly suggests.

At home, Leo runs to his room and gets his money box. He opens it and flips out the content. Together, Leo and Lilly count the money. "Leo, you've already saved $ 20.00 so far," says Lilly. "How long do I have to save?" asks Leo. "You only need $ 10.00. That means you have to help me 5 more times, since you get $ 2.00 for each time you help me, " Lilly explains. "Oh, that is still a long time away," Leo grumbles.
"How about if you come three times a week, then it's even faster."
"Oh yes, Lilly, I'll do that."

The next day after school, Leo goes directly to the company with his dad. He sits down at his own small desk in Lilly's office. And huh, there is already a note. Leo looks at the note carefully. "First, watering flowers; Second, throw letters into the mailbox…" follow by a number of other tasks.

"Lilly, I do not like watering flowers," Leo complains.

"Leo, at work, sometimes you have to do things that are not so much fun," Lilly explains.

"OK," says Leo somewhat annoyed. He begins to throw the letters into the mailboxes. When he finishes, he goes back to his desk and picks up his coloring book.

Lilly asks, "Leo, have you completed all your tasks?"

"Oh," thinks Leo. He forgot to water the flowers and do the other tasks.

"I'll do it tomorrow. I'd rather paint now!"

"Think about your scooter!" Lilly reminded her brother. "If you do not complete your tasks, you won't get $ 2.00 from me."

"I do not want to," Leo said angrily.

Leo and Lilly's parents come to their office to pick them up and go home.

Leo was in a really bad mood on the way home. Slowly he realizes that today he did not get his $ 2.00 and can save nothing. "Darn, now it will take even longer before I can buy my scooter," Leo thinks sadly.

Lilly turns to Leo. "Look Leo. If you set yourself a goal, like buying the scooter, you have to try to stick to it. Hold on until you reach the finish. Some days this might be quite exhausting, and it is not always fun. But Leo, I believe in you, you can do it!" Lilly says confidently. Leo likes to hear this and now he is sure he can.

The next few days pass by as if in flight. Leo works hard and helps Lilly as promised. One night, Lilly asks her little brother, "Leo, why don't we count together how much money you have already saved."

"Oh yes!" Leo rejoices and runs to get his money box. He shakes the box first and then he tips out the money. "Wow, that's a lot," he says with bright eyes. Quickly they count the money.

"Leo, you did it. You saved enough to buy the scooter," Lilly says proudly. "Yippy ..!" Leo calls cheerfully and runs back and forth in the room.

Lilly calls him, "Leo, your endurance has paid off! Tomorrow after school, we'll go together to buy the scooter! "

The next day, Lilly picks Leo up from school. As promised, the two go to the scooter shop. Leo is very excited and happy. In the scooter shop, Leo storms to his new scooter. The new scooter is so beautiful!
Together Lilly and Leo go to the cash desk. "I would like to buy this scooter from my own saved money," says Leo full of joy and gives the cashier his money.

"Did you save all this money by yourself for the scooter?" asks the cashier amazed. Leo smiled proudly and nodded. "I hope you have a lot of fun with your new scooter!" says the cashier kindly and gives Leo his scooter.

At home, he quickly puts on his helmet and runs outside to Maya and the other children. "Look, Maya, my own scooter. I bought it with my own saved money." "That is great, Leo!" Maya rejoices for Leo. Maya and Leo run off with their scooters. They spend the whole afternoon together and have great fun.

www.ingramcontent.com/pod-product-compliance
Lightning Source LLC
Chambersburg PA
CBHW040033050426
42453CB00003B/106